ABANDONED
NORTHERN
NEW JERSEY

ABANDONED
NORTHERN
NEW JERSEY

HOMAGE TO LOST DREAMS

CINDY VASKO

AMERICA
THROUGH TIME®
ADDING COLOR TO AMERICAN HISTORY

I dedicate this book to Andrew Straatveit and Liz Roll for their relentless and ultimately successful endeavors to rescue me from the collateral damage of my brief residency in a Northern New Jersey sinkhole.

America Through Time is an imprint of Fonthill Media LLC
www.through-time.com
office@through-time.com

Published by Arcadia Publishing by arrangement with Fonthill Media LLC
For all general information, please contact Arcadia Publishing:
Telephone: 843-853-2070
Fax: 843-853-0044
E-mail: sales@arcadiapublishing.com
For customer service and orders:
Toll-Free 1-888-313-2665

www.arcadiapublishing.com

First published 2020

Copyright © Cindy Vasko 2020

ISBN 978-1-63499-236-7

Typeset in Trade Gothic 10pt on 15pt
Printed and bound in England

CONTENTS

INTRODUCTION

Memento mori—*Remember, You Are Mortal*

U rban explorers are the lucky observers of cultural deterioration and neglect. Urban explorers differentiate from tourists who visit ancient ruins of a distant, unfamiliar past, in that urban explorers view the beginnings of often-planned contemporary obsolescence.

I was always drawn to stories of times lost—ancient and modern-day. I find the vestiges of abandoned sites captivating, especially when a ruin's cloak of deterioration holds nature's hand—themes of evanescence and mortality embrace abandonments. A forlorn structure's patina hints at hidden histories, but fundamentally reveal a central reminder that all must return to nature. In essence, all ruins put us in our place, or, *memento mori*—remember: you are mortal.

Can you comprehend the stillness of an abandoned building? Do you sense the unresolved history? Imagine nature sluggishly swallowing a structure's bones. *Memento mori* is not meant to be morose, but to inspire, motivate, and clarify. I hope my photographs act as *memento mori*—to remind us that everything has an end, but that one should enjoy and nurture everything while it lasts. In such derelict settings, one can envision what an environment would look like if humans disappeared from the earth. Such apocalyptic scenarios are simultaneously disturbing and fascinating. Perhaps we need to witness such landscapes, to enjoy what we have and the time in front of us.

On the one hand, my photos present an environmental statement where one observes how humans create massive garbage pits and waste on the foundations of derelict structures; while on the other hand, the message reveals how nature can be strong and beautiful when humanity is absent. In much of my photography, silent comments about economic disinvestment prevail with attempts to capture the few remaining memories of a desolate site. The conscientious urban explorer, therefore, seeks to create a relationship with the past and reveal a history not yet sanitized by the wrecking ball.

My book holds representations of abandoned sites that were once in caring hands. Life endured in these environments. People worked in these settings, and perhaps some died in these places. Even though some of these derelict spaces might be dilapidated, vandalized, or collapsed, they endure as settings of beauty. The grace of abandonments remains even with peeling paint and missing windows. Fortunately, several sites I present in this book are renewed or are under the process of revitalization with their proud chronicles deserving of an enduring platform.

A reader can travel to past times with me and view remarkable history and envision his or her own stories of Northern New Jersey's honorable past. Discover the accounts about the Fort Hancock sentinels along the Sandy Hook shoreline, to two jewels of our proud national heritage crown, Ellis Island Hospital Complex, and the Central Railroad of New Jersey Terminal at Liberty Park. Completing the historical and pictorial dialogue are stories about a peculiar pump house and a decimated hospital that once served tubercular and geriatric psychiatric patients. Imagine your own stories when you view my photographs and read their history.

1

ELLIS ISLAND HOSPITAL COMPLEX

E llis Island is the jewel of our national heritage crown—the gateway to the U.S. for millions of immigrants in the late nineteenth and early twentieth centuries. The Ellis Island Immigration Station, now a museum, is the structure most identify when they recall immigrants arriving in the U.S. During its sixty-two years of operation, about 12 million immigrants passed through the Immigration Station. Opposite the Immigration Station, however, is Ellis Island's General Hospital and Contagious Disease Hospital complex. The importance of Ellis Island's Hospital compound is significant. The hospital provided care for those in need of medical attention, and it was the barrier to any diseases possibly establishing grips on the U.S. mainland.

Furthermore, immigrants were born on Ellis Island and some died there. While 12 million immigrants viewed Ellis Island as a beacon of hope and dreams, 3,500 immigrants experienced the site as an island of sadness, with their untimely passing within its walls. While a constant stream of immigrants arrived in the early twentieth century, the Ellis Island Hospital examined immigrants before allowing permission to step foot on the mainland. Here, within the view of the Statue of Liberty and its celebrated symbolism, the hospital delivered babies and attended to the sick, while some faced death and others were forced to return to their homeland.

Even though the hospital closed in 1930, some activity remained on the island for a few decades, but after 1950, all structures were abandoned, and the hospital buildings and contents were left at the mercy of nature's force. After decades of neglect, attempts to arrest the decay commenced with the removal of decaying interior artifacts and installation of vented windows. The good people of the Save Ellis Island Foundation have since stepped in with grand efforts for the preservation of our nation's legacy.

The Ellis Island Hospital complex on the south side of the island embraces twenty-two buildings that once attended to medical specialties, including contagious diseases, psychiatry, and any medical vocation requiring assistance for the inflow of immigrants to the U.S. more than a century ago. The hospital was the first public health hospital in the U.S. Advanced for its time, the hospital incorporated the latest state of the art medical treatments and medical practices, such as fluoroscopy and the use autoclaves for mattress sterilization. Additionally, the complex was also a teaching hospital and attracted experts domestically and internationally.

I am the great-granddaughter of a Lithuanian immigrant that stepped foot on Ellis Island in the early days of the twentieth century. My great-grandmother often spoke of her Ellis Island experiences and her story of a quest for a better life. Her story mirrors other immigrants' accounts, as tens of millions of Americans today are descendants of such immigrants.

My great-grandmother purchased a tiny metal replica of the Statue of Liberty at the 1939 New York World's Fair and proudly displayed it in her house. My great-grandmother proclaimed this tiny statue as her favorite trinket because the grand lady with the torch appeared unexpectedly when she finally emerged from the dreary steerage section of the steamship that transported her to the U.S. She was one of the tired and poor, among the huddled mass cramped in the third-class area of the steamship traveling from Lithuania to America. Third-class steamship travel was a dark and dank place, with hundreds of people crammed into a small space—men, women, and children, so many of whom were ill. My great-grandmother's journey required two weeks to cross the ocean, although she said she lost count of the days within the ever-present gloom of the ship.

After the long voyage to the U.S., however, my great-grandmother and the others emerged from the steamship's darkness, and with the painful, but welcomed brightness of daylight, saw a beautiful woman with a lamp in her hand. My great-grandmother added that there was so much crying and moaning from the collective within the depths of the ship during the sea crossing, but once the Statue of Liberty was in sight of the travelers, there was nothing but silence and reverence. My great-grandmother often laughed about the massive size of Lady Liberty's hands, just like hers. Yes, my great-grandmother's hands were extraordinarily large and strong. She came to the Promised Land alone at the tender age of sixteen, with her large hands pledged to a strange man, and eventually, seven children. Years later, some of her family journeyed to America, but many of her family remained in Lithuania. With so many family members exiled to Siberia at the time of Stalinist Soviet Union, my great-grandmother lost contact with her kinfolk. Several family members faced incarceration in Vilnius, Lithuania, as a result of their political affiliations, and some died during imprisonment because of their partisan attachments. I recently learned that many of my twentieth-century exiled Lithuanian family members bravely escaped

Siberia and returned to their beloved Lithuania. My Lithuanian family descendants are happy and thriving in their homeland, thanks to their adventurous and tenacious spirit—the same resolve my great-grandmother possessed when she stepped foot on Ellis Island and rooted my American family.

Curiously, some, including my great-grandmother's perception, identify Ellis Island as a New York territory without realizing that part of it—actually, most of it—is New Jersey territory. I am unable to recall any immigrant stories that speak of sailing a ship across the seas to Ellis Island in New Jersey. Both New Jersey and New York claim Ellis Island territory. In the late 1990s, the Supreme Court finally settled the question of Ellis Island ownership, but achieving this end required travel along a quarrelsome legal road.

For several centuries, the nebulous language of a seventeenth-century land endowment was at issue, with both New York and New Jersey asserting Ellis Island as their own. The land grant from the English duke of York in 1664 established an English colony situated between the Delaware River, the Hudson River, and the Atlantic Ocean. New Jersey's title was delimited on the east part of the Atlantic Ocean and, in part, by the Hudson River. New Jersey officials assumed this language afforded New Jersey's entitlement to the western half of the Hudson River, which would include Ellis Island, while New York believed it owned the Hudson River islands.

A construction accident in 1986 finally forced the issue of possession on a journey to the Supreme Court. In 1986, the federal government was overseeing Ellis Island's construction activity when a worker lost a leg in an accident during the renovation of the Immigration Museum. The injured construction worker filed a claim against the company that manufactured the equipment causing him to lose his leg. The manufacturer, in turn, sued the federal government for a portion of the accident liability. The federal government, however, preferred the island ownership to be in New Jersey's hands since the federal government perhaps had a better chance of evading a lawsuit under New Jersey law. The federal government attempted to hand over the land to New Jersey, but New York refused to accept this action. The New York Federal District Court in Manhattan and the Second Circuit Court of Appeals reaffirmed that Ellis Island belonged to New York. Of course, New Jersey stepped in with a protest of this ruling and appealed to the Supreme Court for a land ownership distinction.

In 1998, the Supreme Court established the title designation in New Jersey *v.* New York. The court ruled that Ellis Island's landfill was New Jersey territory, as New Jersey owned part of the river to the island. Since the island's landfill was on top of New Jersey's portion of river mass, New Jersey owned more than 20 acres of landfill. The state of New York could maintain its claim to the first island—about 17 percent of the island, or about 5 acres, including the Ellis Island museum. The other areas, though, were New Jersey possessions, including the hospital complex. A few buildings, however, are divided—some reside in both New York and New Jersey.

Did such New York or New Jersey boundary distinctions matter to the brave immigrants traveling to the U.S. for a new life? Of course not, as a state distinction was irrelevant to those leaving their beloved birthplaces and toiling on the steamships in search of a better future. My great-grandmother was a proud American once she acquired her citizenship, and all states are part of the whole—the collective greatness of America. My great-grandmother never referred to herself as a New Yorker, or even a Pennsylvanian, where she settled. She was simply and plainly an American. We must not turn our backs on our shared history, and this caveat is even more salient today than it has been in previous decades. We are a nation of immigrants—all of us. Indeed, new studies reveal that even the ancestors of Native Americans traveled across the continents to our indigenous soil by way of the now-submerged Bering landmass, which in ancient times connected the Russian Far East and distant North America. We must come together and realize that we are all a part of something from somewhere else. We share this diversity, and it is such diversity that weaves into the richness, and uniqueness, of our country. Just like the immigrants of the late nineteenth and early twentieth century arriving at Ellis Island, hopes and dreams never cease, nor should compassion for those escaping persecution or poverty, for such issues are morally crystal clear when we embrace our history.

IMMIGRATION INSPECTION STATION/MUSEUM: The Immigration Station is photographed from the south side Ellis Island Immigrant Hospital. The Immigration Station Museum is operated by the National Park Service and opened in 1892.

HOSPITAL AS SEEN FROM NORTH SIDE OF ELLIS ISLAND: Part of an immigrant's processing at Ellis Island required a physical exam that often was just a brief visual scan as the immigrants stepped foot on the island.

CONTAGIOUS DISEASE HOSPITAL PAVILIONS: A maze of connecting corridors and wards had patients partitioned by disease type, including tuberculosis, scarlet fever, measles, and more.

FERRY BUILDING CORRIDOR TO CONTAGIOUS DISEASE HOSPITAL COMPLEX: The Ferry Building served as an immigrant waiting area. Those passing the health inspection awaited Ferry Building boats to New Jersey or New York.

HOSPITAL LAUNDRY WASHING MACHINE: The laundry building washed and sanitized over 3,000 pieces of laundry each day.

SMITH DRUM WASHING MACHINE: The hospital held two steam-powered machines, a water extractor, and a large press called a mangle.

▲ **LAUNDRY BUILDING:** Since antibiotics were unavailable when the hospital opened, industrial washing machines were necessary to eradicate the bacteria on patient gowns and bedding linens.

▼ **AUTOCLAVE:** A machine called an autoclave sterilized mattresses. The mattress was steam boiled for the elimination of bacteria.

▲ **STAIRCASE:** Ellis Island's busiest period occurred during the pre-World War I years. In 1907, over 1 million immigrants arrived on the island.

▼ **HOSPITAL BUILDING CORRIDOR EXTERIOR:** Most of the patients arriving at Ellis Island were economically disadvantaged and immigrated to the U.S. for employment in physically challenging jobs.

CONTAGIOUS DISEASE PAVILION CORRIDOR: Cove edging on the floors and ceilings, as well as painted plaster walls, provided efficient means for cleaning and sanitizing hospital space.

CONTAGIOUS DISEASE PAVILION: Immigrants feared the last examination of the health assessment, as physicians used a buttonhook to invert eyelids for eye inspections and signs of trachoma.

ANTIQUE FIRE EXTINGUISHER AND CART: Children over twelve years old deemed too ill to enter the U.S. returned to their home country by themselves, whereas ill children under twelve returned to their home country with one parent.

PATIENT ROOM: Immigrants traveling in the ship's steerage area were visually inspected at Ellis Island, and about one in five were pulled for additional medical evaluation.

▲ **MORGUE:** During the hospital's service, 3,500 patients passed away.

▼ **AUTOPSY AMPHITHEATER:** The autopsy amphitheater included the morgue and held the cadavers awaiting autopsies. This area featured a teaching/lecture hall setting for medical students, and physicians from across the U.S. and from other countries.

▲ EXTERIOR OF BUILDING IN CONTAGIOUS DISEASE SECTION:
The contagious disease section included the powerhouse and laundry building.

▼ CONTAGIOUS DISEASE WARD:
The contagious disease complex held eight measles wards. Most infectious illnesses, though, did not automatically prevent an immigrant from entering the U.S. If an immigrant recovered from an affliction, he or she would return for immigration processing to the mainland.

◄ **CONTAGIOUS DISEASE PAVILION OPERATING ROOM:** Island Three held the contagious disease pavilions, along with their operating rooms. The general hospital is on Island Two.

▶ **ENTRANCE TO PATIENT WARD:** The hospital held about 450 beds and about fourteen patients were in each patient room.

▲ TUBERCULOSIS WARD WITH VIEW OF STATUE OF LIBERTY IN THE MIRROR: The tuberculosis ward was an isolation area with private rooms. Each private room included two sinks—one for sputum removal and one for washing.

▼ CONTAGIOUS DISEASE HOSPITAL CONNECTING CORRIDOR: During a contagious disease outbreak, the patients and hospital staff were quarantined within the ward for up to three weeks.

◄ **EXTERIOR DOORWAY TO CONTAGIOUS DISEASE PAVILLION:** As immigrants stepped foot on Ellis Island, the doctors made a health assessment, often within six seconds, as to whether the immigrants were healthy enough to work in the U.S.

▶ **DOORWAY TO CONNECTED ROOMS IN CHIEF PHYSICIAN'S LIVING QUARTERS:** The primary doctors of Ellis Island, such as the chief of surgery and the chief of psychiatry, lived with their families in apartments located at the end of the hospital complex.

◀ **PHYSICIAN RESIDENCE:** Because Ellis Island immigrants arrived from all continents, many domestic and international physicians visited the hospital to assess maladies not previously seen.

▶ **PATIENT WARD:** Incoming immigrants believed to be medical risks received an affliction-identifying chalk-marked letter on their clothes. Representative examples included "X" for insanity, "P" for pulmonary problems, "Pg" for pregnancy, and "Ct" for eye disease.

▲ **CORRIDOR TO PATIENT WARD:** Isolation wards were at the end of the Island and closest to the Statute of Liberty. Terminal immigrants or those awaiting deportation often had rooms with the better views.

▼ **ROOM DEDICATED TO ANIMAL TESTING:** Approximately 10 percent of Ellis Island immigrants were hospitalized. The average hospital stay for treatable afflictions was two weeks.

◄ **ROOM DEDICTED TO ANIMAL TESTING:** By the early 1900s, Ellis Island expanded from 3.3 acres of natural land to 27.5 acres, courtesy of landfill.

► **CONTAGIOUS DISEASE WARD:** Autopsies were required if an immigrant died in the hospital.

CONTAGIOUS DISEASE PAVILION CORRIDOR: Pavilion hospital design embraced the importance of airflow and incorporated small ventilation openings beneath the windowsills. The ventilation system also prevented air from traveling between floors.

FERRY VIEW OF ELLIS ISLAND SOUTH SIDE HOSPITAL COMPLEX: Once immigrants passed the health examination and further processing, they received a "landing card"—a permit to leave Ellis Island and enter the U.S. mainland.

2

CENTRAL RAILROAD OF NEW JERSEY TERMINAL AT LIBERTY STATE PARK

The Father of Liberty State Park and Fighter for Just Causes

Epitaph on Morris Pesin's gravestone

The Central Railroad of New Jersey ("CRRNJ") Terminal in Liberty State Park presents a glimpse into Northern New Jersey's industrial past. Forming a beautiful architectural triumvirate with Ellis Island and the Statue of Liberty, the renovation of the interior of the terminal and its concourse is complete, although no longer in use as a train terminal. Liberty State Park, along with its historical structures, is a new American landmark and also one of the best examples of urban environmental restoration. The park, developed from land once used by the railroad industry, also claims history as one of America's most active transportation centers.

From 1889–1967, the site of Liberty State Park was the hub for the Lehigh Valley, CRRNJ, and Baltimore and Ohio Railroads. The CRNNJ Terminal building is a stunning piece of architecture and was the recipient of restoration funding after it incurred significant damage during 2012's Superstorm Sandy. Constructed in 1889, the CRRNJ Terminal served as the main passenger terminal for the CRRNJ for over eighty years. The CRRNJ Terminal, one part of the momentous trilogy of America's immigration heritage, joins the Statue of Liberty and Ellis Island for a seal on our nation's legacy. While immigrants in search of the American dream arrived in the U.S. by steamship and were welcomed to America by the sight of the Statue of Liberty and received immigration processing and health inspections at Ellis Island, two-thirds of these immigrants proceeded to the CRRNJ Terminal for further destinations in the U.S. and the dawn of their new lives.

When approaching the CRRNJ Terminal parking lot by car, the first thing one notices is the Abraham Lincoln Bush-designed train rain shed next to the terminal.

During a significant CRRNJ Terminal expansion in 1913, the rain shed's primary function was to keep rail passengers protected from the elements as they stepped on and off the trains. The vast renovated concourse connecting the rain shed with the terminal was also constructed at this time. With the concourse and train terminal restored to their former majesty, the rain shed continues to decay.

Thanks to inconvenience and the subsequent vision afforded to a Jersey City businessman, the grandeur of Liberty State Park is a gift to Northern New Jersey and our nation. In 1957, Morris Pesin—businessman, lawyer, councilman, and activist—and his family embarked on a grueling three-hour trip for a visit to the Statue of Liberty. The destination required a difficult drive through the Holland Tunnel for access to a boat at New York City's Battery Park dock that would take the family to the Statue of Liberty. The route Pesin and his family traveled was the only option for an outing to the Statue of Liberty.

Because of the unforeseen three-hour traffic journey, the Pesin family missed their boat when they arrived at the Lower Manhattan Battery Park dock. While standing in Battery Park, Pesin grabbed a glimpse of the desolate, decaying New Jersey shoreline and its rotting piers. While viewing this, Pesin experienced an epiphany with a call to action for the resurrection and clearing of this New Jersey land tract, as New Jersey's shoreline/landmass is only one-half mile to the Statue of Liberty. Shortly after this experience, Pesin undertook a short eight-minute canoe ride to Liberty Island. An editor from the *Jersey Journal* newspaper accompanied Pesin in the canoe. This brief canoe excursion brought forth attention and action for cleanup of the shoreline area, now known as Liberty State Park. Pesin wanted a proper backdrop for an essential symbol of our nation, as well as a more reasonable route for an excursion to the Statue of Liberty, especially for New Jersey residents. The blighted, polluted heap of metal waste along the shoreline was transformed into a beautiful green space for recreational activities and, most importantly, included additional ferry service to the Statue of Liberty and Ellis Island. Liberty State Park opened during America's 1976 bicentennial year—a fitting, patriotic tribute to our honored heritage.

CENTRAL RAILROAD OF NEW JERSEY TERMINAL: The Central Railroad of New Jersey's passenger terminal in Jersey City, New Jersey, is also known as Communipaw Terminal and Jersey City Terminal.

RAIN SHED AT CENTRAL RAILROAD OF NEW JERSEY TERMINAL: The rain shed was built in 1913 during a major terminal expansion. The primary function of the shed was to protect rail passengers from nature's elements once they stepped on and off the trains.

NORTH SIDE OF TERMINAL WITH RAIN SHED IN FOREGROUND: The rain shed at the Terminal is the largest rain shed ever built with dimensions of 400 feet wide by over 800 feet long.

TERMINAL CLOCK: The clock on the front of the terminal includes the words "Industry," "Science," "Agriculture," and "Commerce."

RAIN SHED: The rain shed contained twenty tracks for service to Manhattan. At its peak, 65,000 people passed through the shed and rode on over 350 trains.

TERMINAL CONCOURSE: The vast concourse connecting to the rain shed and terminal was constructed in 1913. The terminal operated until 1967.

RAIN SHED: The agency that governs and operates Liberty State Park, the New Jersey Department of Environmental Protection, is considering historical preservation or demolition of the shed.

RAIN SHED: At one time, the sprawling railroad operations operated along the Jersey City waterfront known as Communipaw Cove.

RAIN SHED (LEFT), TERMINAL CONCOURSE (CENTER), TERMINAL (REAR): A. Lincoln Bush designed the rain shed; it is the largest rain shed ever constructed in the U.S.

RAIN SHED: At one time, the rain shed covered twelve platforms and twenty rail tracks.

RAIN SHED COLUMN: The rain shed, along with the terminal, docks, and yards, was one of several massive industrial complexes that dominated the western New York harbor from the mid-nineteenth to the mid-twentieth century.

AREA ONCE DEDICATED TO TERMINAL FERRY DOCKS: The Communipaw ferry was once the main ferry route from the terminal and operated four ferries that traveled to lower Manhattan. The Manhattan skyline is in the background.

AREA ONCE DEDICATED TO TERMINAL FERRY DOCKS: The origins of Liberty Park are within the transportation sector. This New Jersey shoreline was a natural staging area for major transportation platforms.

▲ **AREA ONCE DEDICATED TO TERMINAL FERRY DOCKS:** At its peak, the area now known as Liberty Park held almost 100 miles of rail while encircling a network of docks and piers.

▼ **DECOMMISSIONED JERSEY CENTRAL LINES TRAIN PARKED AT TERMINAL:** By the turn of the twentieth century, the Central Railroad of New Jersey Terminal accommodated between 30,000 and 50,000 people per day on 128 ferry runs and 300 trains.

EMPTY SKY MEMORIAL WITH TWO CROSSED BEAMS FROM THE FALLEN WORLD TRADE CENTER: Empty Sky is New Jersey's memorial to 749 people that lived in or had ties to New Jersey and lost their lives at the World Trade Towers on September 11, 2001. The brushed stainless steel twin walls rise 30 feet.

NO TRESSPASSING: A rusted no trespassing sign is affixed to the abandoned rain shed.

3

FORT HANCOCK

W alls, along with their purposes, fill today's news headlines and were essential security barriers for much of our nation's past military defense strategies. Impenetrable walls were crucial design elements for a fort. Some of America's rich military history is encased within its imposing forts, and this is obvious when one notices the many forts and garrisons dotting the American landscape. Since colonial times, forts were strategically constructed to monitor the various seacoasts, waterways, harbors, towns, and other military locations. Several forts were important strongholds and served as centers for coastal defense during the American Revolution, War of 1812, Civil War, Spanish-American War, as well as World Wars I and II. Later, some military forts acted as sentinels during the Cold War with the Soviet Union. Some fortresses are preserved in arrested decay; some are in ruins and continue to deteriorate; while others still serve as operational military facilities.

Sandy Hook is a 6-mile-long peninsula projecting from the New Jersey coast into the Atlantic Ocean at the northern end of Jersey's Monmouth County. Even though Sandy Hook is now a lively recreational site, for many years, Sandy Hook, along with its Fort Hancock, served as the venue for military operations. Because of Sandy Hook's proximity to New York City and her waterways, the Hook's location was an ideal platform for defense of the New York metropolis and its harbors. For a successful attack upon the New York harbor, enemy warships would have to navigate the Sandy Hook Channel and would be within short cannon range of Sandy Hook's shoreline. Before the current activities of swimming, sunbathing, fishing, and surfing, the Hook's beaches featured army drills and target practice with heavy artillery. Throughout this landscape, one can still see the vestiges of imposing defense batteries, mortars, and weapon transport tracks.

The U.S. Army deactivated Fort Hancock at Sandy Hook Unit Gateway National Recreation Area more than four decades ago when it exchanged authoritative hands with the U.S. National Park Service. The Park Service continues its search for renovation solutions for the vacant fort structures and buildings marking this fort footprint.

The construction of Fort Hancock was completed in 1895. The fortification of this strategic area was overdue since Sandy Hook was devoid of military buttressing during the American Revolution and War of 1812. During the American Revolution, British troops were able to enter the New York Harbor unopposed. Similarly, with the War of 1812, the British Navy blockaded the harbor of New York. The War of 1812 exposed significant vulnerabilities in defense and thus warranted a defense of maritime ports with permanent and reliable fortifications. In 1859, the U.S. Army Engineers commenced the construction of a massive, granite masonry fort at the north end of Sandy Hook. Before the completion of the masonry fort, however, rifled artillery was introduced into America's arsenal. The new technology of rifled artillery pulverized brick and granite walled forts, thus sending many types of fortifications, including the Fort Hancock's new citadel, into immediate obsolescence. Fort Hancock's engineering design table prompted the implementation of new plans featuring concrete barricades to overcome these defense liabilities.

While Fort Hancock was undergoing construction, the U.S. Army's first proving ground at Sandy Hook materialized in 1874 to test new weapons and artillery. The Sandy Hook Proving Ground served as a weapons test site until 1919 when weapons testing relocated to the Aberdeen Proving Ground in Aberdeen, Maryland. Because the New York Harbor was America's most important port, Sandy Hook was the site for America's first concrete gun batteries. Moreover, the army constructed its first, and only, steam-powered lift-gun battery with Hancock's Battery Potter. Battery Potter was completed in 1895 and was also the site of the first mortar battery. A few years later, more gun and mortar batteries, as well as a bakery, mess halls, fire station, post office, hospital, stables, and officers' row, complimented the Fort Hancock footprint.

During World War II, a nine-gun battery joined the Fort Hancock panorama. Later, the Sandy Hook area and Fort Hancock acted as a base for Nike surface-to-air missiles as well as its inclusion in a line of defense of Cold War-era installations along the East Coast of the United States. The National Park Service now oversees the maintenance of the Nike-Ajax and Nike-Hercules Missile Site. Even though the missiles are deactivated and non-operational, the old equipment, radar, missile cases, and launch platforms are still present.

Sandy Hook's Fort Hancock was demilitarized in the mid-1970s. Since this time, the fort's structures have fallen into a state of decrepitude. Once, the houses on officers' row were bustling with activity, but now are silent and decaying. The battlements of the fort are crumbling and hold silent witness to battles never seen. The fort still feels like a military base with lovely paths, roadways, and impressive defense structures. The rows of identical officer housing are always beautiful and colorful.

Why did forts lose their luster for military defense? With the rise of mobile warfare at the beginning of World War II, the resultant speed and reach of artillery and air power of modern weaponry ensured almost any target could be located and destroyed with sufficient force massed against it. The concept of permanency joining with fortified strongholds, such as walls, is a misnomer in much of today's military logic. Curiously, the arguments about walled security dominate our news headlines, and perhaps one only has to look at the many silent forts within the U.S. borders to comprehend the breaks of reason in a present-day hard material perimeter security argument.

DECOMMISSIONED NIKE SURFACE-TO-AIR MISSILE AND COLLAPSED UTILITY BUILDING: During the Cold War, Fort Hancock was the site of a surface-to-air Nike missile base.

MORTAR BATTERY ENTRANCE: The McCook Mortar Battery was completed in 1895. This mortar battery is one of two symmetrical halves.

▲ **STEEL DOOR IN MORTAR PIT AREA:**
Mortars can be shot vertically into the air so
that shells fall on to lightly protected boat
decks or explode in the air raining shrapnel
upon an enemy.

▼ **MORTAR PIT:** Mortars were installed in
ground-level pits surrounded by high walls.
Each of the two mortar pits had four mortars
that allowed the launching of 12-inch, rifled
shells, each weighing 1,000 pounds.

MORTAR PIT ENTRANCE: Other than the mortar pits and entryways, the mortar battery was completely covered with earth for concealment from the enemy.

HIGH STONE WALLS IN FRONT OF MORTAR BATTERY ENTRANCES: The only way for an enemy to disable a mortar pit was to launch mortars of its own, but enemy ships during the late nineteenth or early twentieth century did not carry mortars.

◄ **MORTAR BATTERY REYNOLDS ENTRANCE AND RAILS FOR TRANSPORTING MORTARS TO THE MORTAR PIT:** Battery Reynolds is the second symmetrical half of the mortar battery area. Artillery rounds from an enemy ship could only hit the sides of the earthen mounds and sand dunes that protected the battery.

► **STEEL DOOR IN MORTAR BATTERY ENTRANCE:** With the introduction of aviation warfare in World War II, mortar batteries were obsolete as planes could drop explosives into mortar pits.

▲ STEEL DOOR IN MORTAR PIT:
During World War II, this mortar battery converted into a communications center and the underground interior areas were subdivided into rooms and offices.

▼ BATTERY GRANGER: Battery Granger, a reinforced concrete coastal gun battery held two 10-inch guns in disappearing mounts. The battery was named after Major General Gordon Granger, a celebrated military figure of the Mexican and the Civil War theaters.

BATTERY POTTER: Battery Potter held America's first and only steam-powered hydraulic lift gun battery. The battery was named after Brigadier General H. Potter who served in the Mexican and Civil War.

MORTARS AT BATTERY POTTER: Battery Potter was transformed into a harbor and defense command post during World War II.

MAINTENANCE BUILDING: During World War I, some guns from Hancock's batteries were removed and sent to France for mounting on rail cars. One gun from the Hancock's nine-gun battery was transported to France.

INTERIOR OF MAINTENANCE BUILDING: Hancock's nine-gun battery is the longest concrete harbor defense gun battery built by the Army.

INTERIOR OF MAINTENANCE BUILDING: In 1940 and the buildup toward World War II, Fort Hancock was federalized with the National Guard and reserve units. Later that year, the draft commenced and draftees arrived at Fort Hancock.

MAINTENANCE BUILDING: As World War II neared its end, the mined New York harbor was cleared, and by the end of 1945, harbor defenses returned to peacetime status and Fort Hancock personnel levels dropped.

▲ MAINTENANCE BUILDING:
Two days after the commencement
of the Korean War, Fort Hancock
was deactivated. The reactivation
of Hancock, however, occurred
during the Cold War when the U.S.
Army deployed a Nike-Ajax missile
system. Later, the Nike-Hercules
missile system was also deployed
at Fort Hancock.

▼ MAINTENANCE BUILDING:
The Nike-Hercules system at Fort
Hancock was formally deactivated
in 1974.

▲ **MAINTENANCE BUILDING:** Steel and concrete fortifications were common during the nineteenth and early twentieth centuries. Advances in modern warfare since World War II, though, made large-scale fortifications obsolete in most situations.

▼ **MAINTENANCE BUILDING:** Fort Hancock is situated on the Sandy Hook Peninsula on the northern tip of Monmouth County. Sandy Hook, now a recreational destination, holds a long history of military functions.

▲ MAINTENANCE BUILDING:
Fort Hancock's close proximity to New York City and her waterways made this section of land a prime location from which to defend New York City and its harbors.

▼ MAINTENANCE BUILDING DOORS:
From 1874 to 1919, Sandy Hook was used as a proving ground for the military's experimental weaponry.

▲ MAINTENANCE BUILDING: Hancock's nine-gun battery was constructed during World War II to guard the water routes to New York City. The enormous fortification was intended to keep the harbor safe from attack by enemy ships and German U-Boats.

▼ HURRICAINE SANDY HIGH WATER MARK: 2012's Superstorm Sandy disabled Fort Hancock's utility system including electricity, telephone/data, and water and waste treatment. In the days after the storm, the fort's maintenance buildings were only accessible by boat.

BATTERY PECK: Within its reinforced concrete walls, Battery Peck held a 6-inch coastal gun. The battery was named after 1Lt. Fremont P. Peck, who was accidentally killed in 1895 by a gun burst at the Sandy Hook Proving Ground.

BATTERY PECK: Battery Peck's construction started in 1901 and completed in 1903.

BATTERY PECK UPPER LEVEL GUN PLATFORM: Battery Peck is a two-story battery with guns on the upper level and a common magazine on the lower level.

BATTERY ALEXANDER: Battery Alexander's reinforced concrete walls held a 12-inch coastal gun. The battery was named after MG William Alexander of the Continental Army for his exemplary service during the Revolutionary War.

▲ **BATTERY ALEXANDER:** Battery Alexander's construction began in 1898 and completed in 1899.

▼ **NINE-GUN BATTERY:** The nine-gun battery contained nine gun emplacements. Initially a six-gun battery, the battery expanded to nine guns and its groups of guns were assigned to four battery names—Alexander, Halleck, Bloomfield, and Richardson.

BATTERY ALEXANDER: Battery Alexander is a part of the nine-gun battery unit.

REAR VIEW OF OFFICERS' HOUSING ALONG OFFICER ROW: Eighteen houses, situated along Sandy Hook Bay, were once the homes of Fort Hancock officers and their families.

BUILDING 23 BARRACKS STRUCTURE: The roof collapsed on the Building 23 Barracks structure. A reconstruction effort of this building as well as others just attained approval. An anticipated renovation of Building 23 is expected in late 2021.

OFFICERS' ROW ALONG SANDY HOOK BAY: Many of the officer homes are deteriorating, but some private individuals and companies renovated a few homes.

4

FORSAKEN HOSPITAL

Dying with One's Rights On

Darold Treffert, 1973, *Journal of the American Medical Association*, describing how laws and regulations might have become too rigid regarding the protection of individual rights at the expense of well-being.

At a landmass highpoint, and overlooking a fertile valley, is a structure that sits like its former patients—in a state of disrepair with little hope in sight. Broken test tubes, tattered, yellowed medical books, and old patient information cards litter cold, dark rooms and hallways. The imagination of sadness stretches into every dark corner of this former tuberculosis and geriatric psychiatric hospital.

The hospital was originally a tuberculosis center when it opened its doors in the early 1900s. In the late 1970s, the facility transitioned into a hospital that focused on treating geriatric mentally ill patients. One of the buildings within the hospital complex footprint, however, was left to waste away sometime during this transition. The hospital is a ruin of its past, with rampant vandalism evident throughout the structure.

Rusted, corroded elevator doors, overturned furniture, absent staircases to upper floors, and wallpaper-sized sheets of institutional colored paint peel from interior walls. So much dirt and surface deterioration collect in the corridors that peaks and valleys of debris form along the pathways. All at once, however, one enters several sun-lit verandas—peaceful areas and cheery escapes from the dreariness positioned in the rear. There is a shift in the atmosphere, where breathing becomes easy, and a lovely view of a valley greets the eyes. The front of the building is dark and bleak, but the other side is hopeful and bright. Unfortunately, the history of institutions such as these does not hold to an optimistic and bright past. Moreover, the plight of grim history does not end once patients exit the hospital doors of the once large and now-shuttered health facilities crisscrossing the U.S.

Before deinstitutionalization of the state hospitals, such institutions realized the needs of those plagued with mental illness, to include medical treatment, therapy, medications, and perhaps vocational training. The policy of state hospital deinstitutionalization has roots in the twentieth-century civil rights movement when many former hospital patients assimilated into mainstream society. Several dynamics pushed the measures for this integration: views that psychiatric hospitals were punishing and callous; the promise of new psychotropic drugs for treatments; and, always in the background, budgetary considerations.

Further, in the 1999 Supreme Court ruling of Olmstead *v*. L.C., mental illness was determined to be not only an illness, but also a disability and, therefore, covered under the Americans with Disabilities Act. Based on this new ruling, all governmental agencies were required to implement practical measures to transfer people with mental illness into community-based treatment—thus, putting an end to large-scale forced institutionalization.

Has the policy in the aftermath of Olmstead resolved the issues of treating citizens with mental illness? While too many people with severe mental illness are still found in deplorable environments, the hope of new drugs has not successfully improved functioning in all patients, and the institutional closings have deluged underfunded community services that are ill-equipped to handle such service pressures. While it is a noble goal to preserve the rights of people with severe mental illness, so many, however, are victims of the revolving door of hospital admissions. An even more extreme situation occurs when barriers to hospital admissions lead to homelessness with too many wandering the streets and at risk for arrest or death. With seemingly no escape from rules and limitations, will such unfortunate souls imprisoned within these Catch-22 situations die with their rights on?

Is there a solution for avoidance of dying with rights on? Barriers to timely treatment appear too formidable. As noted, during the twentieth century, homelessness associated with those holding severe mental illness became a national issue when state mental hospitals across the nation sealed their doors. At the same time, funds for promised community resources languished. Decades later, the psychiatric system continues to suffer from a lack of treatment beds and subsidies. Additionally, administrative and legal barriers often thwart treatment for mental illness. Noble intentions, such as the concept that patients must hit rock bottom or volunteer for treatment, often result in too many patients too ill to seek help.

Perhaps state hospitals must return to their traditional role of a hospital of last resort? Perhaps state hospitals must re-emerge, as entry points for those holding acute mental illness that otherwise will find themselves incarcerated or living on the streets? So many comprehensive health facilities are abandoned and rot along the American landscape. These institutions, however, still hold the historical demons of abuse and cloud any prospect of effective, humane reform toward a repurpose of these facilities. Adequate housing with various degrees of compassionate supervision and facilities holding a full-compliment of assistance must merge with the mental health system before revisits to large health care facilities are realities. Revised laws and regulations allowing for access to needed health care services should be implemented for appropriate care of this disadvantaged population, so these unfortunate citizens do not die with their rights on.

▲ REAR EXTERIOR STAIRCASE:
The hospital dates to the early 1900s
when the state opened the tuberculosis
sanatorium in a rural area.

▼ PHARMACY AREA: The hospital
shut down in the 1970s and was left to
deteriorate.

▲ DESK WITH OXYGEN CANISTERS, PAPERWORK, AND PHARMACY BOTTLES: The hospital was able to treat 500 tubercular patients annually when it opened.

▼ PHARMACY AREA: In the late 1920s, more than 10,000 tubercular people were treated.

◄ **DOORWAY:** When the hospital first opened, it would only accept curable tubercular patients, but by the 1920s, the hospital accepted any tubercular patient devoid of severity concerns.

► **PAPERWORK AND SYRINGES:** After new tuberculosis treatments emerged in 1950, the sanatorium widened its treatment plans to include diseases of the chest.

▲ **HALLWAY:** In the late 1970s, a geriatric psychiatric hospital was constructed next to the abandoned sanatorium.

▼ **AUTOPSY TABLE:** The tuberculosis sanatorium was viewed as a model health institution when it opened in the early 1900s.

▲ **VERANDA:** Verandas are found throughout the facility and were helpful to facilitate fresh air treatment for tubercular patients.

▼ **PATIENT WARD:** Tubercular treatment remained relatively unchanged until the introduction of streptomycin in the 1950s.

VERANDA FURNITURE: With the introduction of streptomycin, the need for isolation hospitals lessened, despite the fact that the new drug treatment for tuberculosis only contributed one part of many in the cure of tuberculosis.

VERANDA: In addition to new tubercular drugs treatment, good nutrition, bed rest as well as isolation were still vital to a cure but the public perception of tuberculosis changed.

◄ **PATIENT ROOM WINDOW:** While tuberculosis mortality rates waned in the 1960s, morbidity rates increased.

► **HALLWAY:** In 1950, the hospital's charge expanded from tuberculosis and included treatments for all chest ailments.

▲ **VERANDA:** In the late 1970s, the hospital converted into a state run nursing home and specifically, a geriatric psychiatric hospital.

▼ **PATIENT WARD:** In 1999, the Supreme Court decision in Olmstead *v.* L.C. indicated that mental illness was a disability and therefore covered under the Americans with Disabilities Act.

▲ **PATIENT BED CALL AND LIGHTING HARDWARE:** After the Olmstead Supreme Court decision, all governmental organizations, not just state hospitals, were required to relocate people with mental illness into community-based treatment facilities and end preventable institutionalization.

▼ **MEDICATION ADMINISTRATION ROOM:** In the past, state hospitals provided for the many needs for people afflicted with severe mental illness, including medication administration, medical treatment, and therapy.

▲ **HALLWAY:** Court decisions, especially Olmstead, limited the capacity of the state to sequester people in hospitals against their will.

▼ **KITCHEN:** Many believe the Olmstead Court decision, and other similar court rulings, introduced a new struggle with the law. On the one hand, there is the need to maintain autonomy and avoid unjust hospitalization, and on the other hand, there is the need to recognize and treat people in the early phase of a disease.

ROOM LEADING TO VERANDA: Since Olmstead, many people with severe mental illness fell through the cracks and fostered a repeated cycle of hospital admissions and/or homelessness.

VERANDA: Medicaid shifted the funding for those afflicted with severe mental illness in state hospitals from a state charge to a shared trust with the federal government.

▲ **PATIENT WARD:** Medicaid created a motivation for states to shutter facilities they financed and transfer patients into community hospitals and nursing homes partly funded by Medicaid and the federal government.

▼ **FORLORN MEDICAL BOOK:** The Omnibus Budget Reconciliation Act of 1981 eliminated direct federal funding for community-based nursing homes that mainly treated patients with mental health problems and mandated the assessment of patients entering nursing homes with assurances of legitimate medical illness.

◄ **HALLWAY:** The Omnibus Budget Reconciliation Act of 1981, forced states to return to the funding of non-nursing homes for the long term care of people with severe mental illness and move people into facilities that were often for profit, and privately owned.

▶ **VERANDA:** The obstacles for proper management of people with severe mental illness are daunting.

PATIENT ROOM: Chronic homelessness for those with severe mental illness emerged as a national concern in the mid-twentieth century.

VERANDA: While state mental hospitals in the aftermath of Olmstead were closed, funds for assured community resources declined and many people with severe mental illness were abandoned to the streets or even prison.

◄ **OFFICE:** Too many administrative and legal barriers often hinder effective management of severe mental illness.

▶ **HALLWAY:** The Olmstead decision noted that unwarranted separation of persons with disabilities constitutes discrimination in violation of Title II of the Americans with Disabilities Act.

PATIENT ROOM: The Supreme Court in Olmstead included nursing homes when the court refers to the word institutions.

VERANDA: Up to the mid-twentieth century, people with severe mental illness received treatment in sizable public organizations or trusted their families for care, with little support from the government.

◄ **PATIENT ROOM:** Until the late 1960s, perceptions of interventionism and fear warranted a separated institutionalized reality for people with disabilities.

► **ENTRANCE TO HOSPITAL FROM VERANDA:** The escalating civil rights movement in the mid-twentieth century powered litigation efforts by disability rights proponents pursuing not only an improvement to the quality of life but also a move from needless institutionalization.

▲ **EXIT TO A VERANDA:** During the mid-twentieth century, there was a rising acknowledgement among specialists that people with severe mental illness could benefit and even flourish in less limiting settings.

▼ **DISCARDED PATIENT WARD AND OFFICE FURNITURE:** The Supreme Court in Olmstead held that public organizations must provide community-based services to disabled people, when services are appropriate and the disable people do not oppose community-based treatment.

5

PHILLIPSBURG PUMP HOUSE

With opened faucets and free-flowing water, it is easy to overlook that long before the water reaches our homes or businesses; it travels a long journey to this destination. Before water runs through pipes to reach cities and towns, it starts in nature. During the late nineteenth century and at the turn of the twentieth century, pump houses were typical fixtures for the supply of water to local populations within rural settings and small towns. A pump house's workings are simple—a building that houses a water system and, at a minimum, the inclusion of a pressure tank and pressure control switch.

A peculiar pump house rests in a discrete setting along the Delaware River in Phillipsburg, New Jersey. Before the construction of this pump house, however, the Phillipsburg Water Company incorporated in 1857 to supply water to the village of Phillipsburg when its population was about 1500. In 1861, the Lehigh Water Company of Easton, Pennsylvania, stepped in to provide water to the town of Phillipsburg. In 1885, the Peoples Water Company of Phillipsburg incorporated and designed a system that pumped water from wells and into a raised reservoir. The pump house in Phillipsburg was the source of this Peoples Water Company system.

The Phillipsburg pump house's reinforced concrete housing holds a remarkable 51-foot-tall water pumping apparatus, also known as Big Alice. Big Alice is a 300-horsepower, vertical, triple-expansion, coal-fired, steam-powered engine manufactured by Allis Chalmers of Milwaukee, Wisconsin. At the peak of pump house operations, Big Alice pushed 6 million gallons of water each day from its wells to a reservoir on nearby Marble Mountain as it served the Phillipsburg community.

The pumping station was operational until 1969 when a new well system of submerged electric pumps went operational. The facility's steam pump was put on backup status and underwent yearly assessment checks until 1982. The pump house is now under the caring hands of the Friends of the New Jersey Transportation

Heritage Center. The heritage center also utilizes the pump house as a storage facility and what is stored within the walls of the pump house is an unexpected wealth of fascinating artifacts, especially to an urban explorer's eye. Additionally, what looks like a salvage yard in and around the pump house is actually a repository for some of the many items owned by Heritage Center. Inside and outside of the pump house are mostly New Jersey transportation-related signs, lampposts, spare parts, rail sections, and vehicles—retained for a future Heritage Center museum.

While the pump house stood for decades like a silent reminder of Phillipsburg's industrial past, in 2018, the Friends of the New Jersey Transportation Heritage Center completed the restoration of the steam-powered engine. The triple-expansion steam engine now asserts operational status and is the largest-working standing steam engine in North America. Perhaps, the heritage center can now focus on showcasing the historical transportation relics in and around the pump house property.

▲ **ALLIS CHALMERS VERTICLE TRIPLE EXPANSION PUMP:** The massive water pump is housed in a reinforced concrete pump house.

▼ **A PORTION OF THE TRIPLE EXPANSION PUMP:** The water pump was built in 1913 to feed water into a reservoir on top of nearby New Jersey's Marble Mountain.

BOILER DOORS AND SMOKE BOXES: The D. M. Dillon Steam Boiler Works smoke boxes originated in Fitchburg, Massachusetts.

ALLIS-CHALMERS PUMP GAUGE PANEL: The Allis Chalmers engine, manufactured in Milwaukee, Wisconsin, holds the builder's plate with the serial number, 1065-1913.

◄ **PORTION OF TRIPLE EXPANSION PUMP:** An 8-foot by 8-foot by 225-foot cistern sits below the pump pit floor. The cistern rests at the approximate level of the river where it collected ground water.

▶ **PIPE CONDUIT FROM TRIPLE EXPANSION PUMP:** The Allis Chalmers, triple-expansion pump engine, probably transferred to Phillipsburg in pieces and by rail. The engine was most likely assembled before the concrete building housing was completed.

RAILROAD CROSSING SIGNS: The Pennsylvania Railroad delivered coal to the pump house with tracks situated at the rear of the pump house.

OVERLOOK TO PUMP ENGINE PIT: The pump house property held housing for the plant engineer and plant fireman.

PRESERVED TRANSPORTATION ARTIFACTS ON PUMP HOUSE PROPERTY: On August 18–19, 1955, tropical storm Diane flooded the pump house engine pit.

CLOCKWISE FROM TOP LEFT:

EXTERIOR DOOR OF PUMP HOUSE: During tropical storm Diane, the pump house flywheels were submerged, with pump house operations requiring suspension.

STEAM PRESSURE GAUGE: In the final years of the pump house operations, the boilers were fitted to replace coal with gas usage.

TRANSPORTATION ARTIFACTS STORED INSIDE PUMP HOUSE: The pump house was used continuously until 1969 when a new well system with submerged electric pumps was put into operation. The pump incurred testing and remained on standby status until 1982.

TRANSPORTATION ARTIFACTS STORED INSIDE PUMP HOUSE: The pump house property is 96 acres.

ARTIFACTS PRESERVED INSIDE THE PUMP HOUSE: Three safes near the pump house boilers were discovered and contained historical records of the water company.

◄ **PRESERVED TRANSPORTATION ARTIFACTS:** An attempt to revive the vertical triple expansion pump in 2006 resulted in serious damage to the vertical triple expansion engine.

► **TRANSPORTATION ARTIFACTS:** On July 28, 2018, the vertical triple expansion engine was activated for the first time since 1982.

ARTIFACTS INSIDE OF THE PUMP HOUSE: With 2018's successful activation of the vertical triple expansion engine, this operating steam pumping engine is the largest in North America.

VINTAGE TANKER TRUCKS RESTING ON PUMP HOUSE PROPERTY: The only other surviving vertical triple expansion pump engine in New Jersey is at the New Milford Pumping Station in Oradell. The New Milford triple expansion pump engine's integrity is in jeopardy.

OLD CHURCH BUS ON PUMP HOUSE PROPERTY: The original equipment, signage, tools, supplies, equipment, and assorted artifacts are held at the pump house for inclusion into a future Heritage Center.

◄ **INTERIOR OF OLD CHURCH BUS ON PUMP HOUSE PROPERTY:** Since the pump house remains in as-built condition, it qualifies for inclusion into the National Register. Various preservation groups are actively seeking this status.

► **TRANSPORTATION ARTIFACTS INSIDE OF THE PUMP HOUSE:** Future campaigns for the Phillipsburg Pump House include displays in a museum setting, tours, and engine operational demonstrations.

BIBLIOGRAPHY

Edgecombe, M., "The Top 10 Secrets of Liberty State Park," Untapped Cities, May 3, 2018, untappedcities.com/2018/05/02/the-top-10-secrets-of-liberty-state-park/10/

Barone, M., "The Lessons of Ellis Island, and Why Things Are Different Today," *Washington Examiner*, September 8, 2016, www.washingtonexaminer.com/the-lessons-of-ellis-island-and-why-things-are-different-today

Berlinner, III, S., "History of Technology Phillipsburg Water Works," SBIII, July 20, 2010, sbiii.com/phh2owks.html

"Bizarre Art Inside Abandoned Sandy Hook Bunker," Weird NJ, 2019, weirdnj.com/stories/abandoned/bizarre-art-inside-abandoned-sandy-hook-bunker/

"Can Battle to Save Fort Hancock Still Be Won?" *Asbury Park Press*, June 1, 2018, www.app.com/story/opinion/columnists/2018/06/01/fort-hancock-sandy-hook-preservation/611909002/

Chan, S., "Ellis Island's Forgotten Hospital," *New York Times*, October 26, 2007, cityroom.blogs.nytimes.com/2007/10/26/ellis-islands-forgotten-hospital/

Cooper, S., "Inside Ellis Island's Immigrant Hospital," *Tablet Magazine*, October 10, 2017, www.tabletmag.com/jewish-life-and-religion/246347/inside-ellis-islands-immigrant-hospital

Dent, J., "NJ Transportation Center Open House," *Railfan*, September 22, 2001, www.railfan.net/lists/rshsdepot-digest/200109/msg00072.html

Ferro, S., "The Time New Jersey Took New York to the Supreme Court to Lay Claim to Ellis Island," *Mental Floss*, March 9, 2018, mentalfloss.com/article/534851/time-new-jersey-took-new-york-supreme-court-lay-claim-ellis-island

"Fort Hancock," The Lostinjersey Blog, April 8, 2009, lostinjersey.wordpress.com/2009/04/08/fort-hancock/

Garbely, R., "Phillipsburg Pump House Engine Is Now Operational!" Liberty Historic Railway, July 31, 2018, www.lhry.org/news/2018/7/31/phillipsburg-pump-house-engine-is-now-operational

"Gateway National Recreation Area: Officer's Row at Fort Hancock," National Park Planner, 2019, npplan.com/parks-by-state/new-york-national-parks/gateway-national-recreation-area-park-at-a-glance/gateway-national-recreation-area-military-sites/gateway-national-recreation-area-military-sites-at-sandy-hook/gateway-national-recreation-area-fort-hancock-walking-tour/gateway-national-recreation-area-officers-housing-at-fort-hancock/

Greenagel, F., "Domestic Architecture in Warren County," *New Jersey Churchscape*, September 2012, njchurchscape.com/Index-Sept2012.html

Greenhouse, L., "The Ellis Island Verdict: The Ruling; High Court Gives New Jersey Most of Ellis Island," *The New York Times*, May 27, 1998, www.nytimes.com/1998/05/27/nyregion/ellis-island-verdict-ruling-high-court-gives-new-jersey-most-ellis-island.html

"Haunted Jersey Shore: Fort Hancock," *Asbury Park Press*, October 30, 2017, www.app.com/story/news/history/2017/10/30/haunted-jersey-shore-fort-hancock/812944001/

Hindash, S., "Then and Now: See How Phillipsburg Has Transformed Over the Years," Lehighvalleylive.com, July 6, 2018, www.lehighvalleylive.com/warren-county/2018/07/then_and_now_see_how_phillipsb.html

"Hurricane Sandy at Sandy Hook—Six Months Later," National Park Service, U.S. Department of the Interior, February 26, 2015, www.nps.gov/gate/learn/news/sandy-sandy-6.htm

Ingall, M, "Inside Ellis Island's Immigrant Hospital," *Tablet Magazine*, October 10, 2017, www.tabletmag.com/jewish-life-and-religion/246347/inside-ellis-islands-immigrant-hospital

"Jersey City/Communipaw Terminal," American-Rails.com, 2019, www.american-rails.com/jct.html

Kamis-Gould, E., *et al.*, "The Impact of Closing a State Psychiatric Hospital on the County Mental Health System and Its Clients," Psychiatry Online, October 1, 1999, ps.psychiatryonline.org/doi/full/10.1176/ps.50.10.1297

Konnemann, K., "The Remnants Of This Abandoned Fort In New Jersey Are Hauntingly Beautiful," Only In Your State, March 18, 2017, www.onlyinyourstate.com/new-jersey/nj-abandoned-fort-hancock/

Koppenhaver, R., "Pointing the Way," *Skylands Visitor Magazine*, 2019, www.njskylands.com/hstranssigns

"Liberty State Park: History," Department of Environmental Protection, January 27, 2005, www.state.nj.us/dep/parksandforests/parks/liberty_state_park/liberty_history.html

Livio, S. K., "Closure of Hagedorn Psychiatric Hospital Has Patients' Families Worried," NJ.com, July 26, 2011

Marton, J., "The Ellis Island South Side Hospitals: a Healthcare Marvel in Decay," Untapped Cities, May 21, 2013, untappedcities.com/2012/05/08/the-ellis-island-south-side-hospitals-a-healthcare-marvel-in-decay/

Neuhauser, A., "Empty Sky' Memorial Remembers Fallen Towers, 746 New Jerseyans," *Woodbridge Patch*, September 11, 2011, patch.com/new-jersey/woodbridge/empty-sky-memorial-remembers-fallen-towers-746-new-jerseyans-9

New Jersey v. New York, 523 U.S. 767 (1998), supreme.justia.com/cases/federal/us/523/767/case.pdf

"Nike Missile Base Tours, Sandy Hook, New Jersey," Roadside America, 2018, www.roadsideamerica.com/story/11152

Petrick, J., "Morris Pesin Had Vision of Great Park," *The Jersey Journal*, June 13, 2001, www.folsp.org/history/pesin_vision.pdf

Phancyfree, "Peoples Water Company: Historic Pump House," *Barclays Travel*, July 27, 2014, www.barclaycardtravel.com/t5/Travel-Stories/Peoples-Water-Company-Historic-Pump-house/ba-p/1028443

"Phillipsburg NJ," Phillipsburg Area Historical Society, 2015, www.phillipsburghistory.com/history.html

"Phillipsburg Pump House," Friends of the New Jersey Transportation Heritage Center, 2018, www.friendsnjthc.org/pumphouse

Pierce, M., "Documentary History of American Water-Works," Water Works History, 2017, www.waterworkshistory.us/NJ/Phillipsburg/.

Postal, S., "Olmstead at 15: The Legacy of a Landmark Case," American Bar Association, September 27, 2018, www.americanbar.org/groups/health_law/publications/aba_health_esource/2014-2015/september/

Raphelson, S., "How The Loss Of U.S. Psychiatric Hospitals Led To A Mental Health Crisis," *NPR*, November 30, 2017, www.npr.org/2017/11/30/567477160/how-the-loss-of-u-s-psychiatric-hospitals-led-to-a-mental-health-crisis

Sebastian, C., "New York's Hospital of Immigrants: Where Hope and Pain Collide," Cable News Network, October 1, 2014, www.cnn.com/2014/10/01/business/ellis-island-hospital-art-exhibition/index.html

Snook, J., "Voluntary Care Alone Won't Solve the Mentally Ill Homeless Crisis," *New York Post*, December 10, 2018, nypost.com/2018/12/10/voluntary-care-alone-wont-solve-the-mentally-ill-homeless-crisis/

Snyder-Hegener, A., "Assessing the Impact of the Olmstead Decision," *Social Work & Society International Online Journal*, 2012, www.socwork.net/sws/article/view/343/680

Spiegelman, A., and J. R., "The Ghosts of Ellis Island," Damiani, 2015

Spies, S., "H-Net Discussion Networks—Query: History of Hagedorn Psychiatric Hospital," Humanities and Social Sciences Net Online, January 9, 2007, lists.h-net.org/cgi-bin/logbrowse.pl?trx=vx&list=h-new-jersey&month=0701&week=b&msg=ILO9%2BcuS16i5fVpM5kiX5Q&user=&pw=

Staff, *amNY*, "Fascinating Facts About Ellis Island," *Am New York*, December 27, 2016, www.amny.com/news/ellis-island-facts-about-the-immigration-center-and-beyond-1.12781876

Stainton, L., "Democrats Call for NJ To Reopen Hagedorn Psychiatric Hospital," *NJ Spotlight*, February 9, 2018

Swenson, B., "Fort Hancock; Coastal Defense Through the Nuclear Age," *Abandoned Country*, November 10, 2014, www.abandonedcountry.com/2014/11/10/fort-hancock-coastal-defense-through-the-nuclear-age/

"Thank You Morris Pesin," *USA Architects*, June 1, 2016, www.usaarchitects.com/article/thank-you-morris-pesin

Upward2Bound, "New Jersey's Abandoned Psychiatric Hospital," Atlas Obscura, July 12, 2017, www.atlasobscura.com/places/new-jerseys-abandoned-hospitals

Vasko, C., *Abandoned New York* (New York: Arcadia Publishing, 2018), pp. 7–24

Wade, L., "Ancient DNA Confirms Native Americans' Deep Roots in North and South America," American Association for the Advancement of Science, November 8, 2019, www.sciencemag.org/news/2018/11/ancient-dna-confirms-native-americans-deep-roots-north-and-south-america

Williams, L., "Long Term Care After Olmstead *v.* L.C.: Will the Potential of the ADA's Integration Mandate Be Achieved?" *Journal of Contemporary Health Law & Policy*, 2000, scholarship.law.edu/cgi/viewcontent.cgi?article=1258&context=jchlp

Wyckoff, G., *History of Phillipsburg, NJ*, Lewis Historical Publishing Company, 1911, history.rays-place.com/nj/war-phillipsburg.htm

Yohanna, D., "Deinstitutionalization of People with Mental Illness: Causes and Consequences," American Medical Association, October 1, 2013, journalofethics.ama-assn.org/article/deinstitutionalization-people-mental-illness-causes-and-consequences/2013-10

Yue, S., "A Return to Institutionalization Despite Olmstead *v.* L.C.—the Inadequacy of Medicare Provider Reimbursement in Minnesota and the Failure to Deliver Home and Community Based Waiver Services," *Law & Inequality: A Journal of Theory and Practice*, University of Minnesota, 2001, scholarship.law.umn.edu/cgi/viewcontent.cgi?referer=https://www.google.com/&httpsredir=1&article=1031&context=lawineq

ABOUT THE AUTHOR

CINDY VASKO was born in Allentown, Pennsylvania, and resides in Arlington, Virginia, near Washington, D.C. For fifteen years, Cindy was the publications manager for a large construction law firm in Northern Virginia; concurrently, she interviewed musicians, wrote articles, and photographed concerts for a music magazine for four years. While Cindy enjoys partaking in all photography genres and is a multi-faceted photographer, she has a passion for abandoned site photography. Cindy is an award-winning photographer, and her works were featured in many gallery exhibitions, including galleries in New York City, Washington, D.C., Philadelphia, Pennsylvania, and Paris, France.